I0796104

IN-DEMAND CAREERS

BE A

SOLAR PHOTOVOLTAIC INSTALLER

by Miles Herman

BrightPoint Press

San Diego, CA

an imprint of ReferencePoint Press, Inc.
Printed in the United States

For more information, contact:
BrightPoint Press
PO Box 27779
San Diego, CA 92198
www.BrightPointPress.com

LIBRARY OF CONGRESS CATALOGING-IN-PUBLICATION DATA

Name: Herman, Miles, author.
Title: Be a solar photovoltaic installer / by Miles Herman.
Description: San Diego, CA: ReferencePoint Press, 2026 | Series: In-demand careers | Audience: Grade 7 to 9 | Includes bibliographical references and index.
Identifiers: ISBN: 9781678211240 (hardcover) | ISBN: 9781678211257 (eBook)
The complete Library of Congress record is available at www.loc.gov.

CONTENTS

AT A GLANCE

- Solar photovoltaic installers are also called PV installers.

- PV installers set up solar photovoltaic systems, or PV systems. These systems convert sunlight into electricity.

- PV installers put in PV systems at homes and businesses. PV systems must meet government building codes.

- Students can take classes to become PV installers. Community colleges, trade schools, and clean energy organizations offer various programs.

- Solar companies may train people to become PV installers. This is called on-the-job training.

- Solar energy is a booming business in the United States. In 2024, the United States had around 10,000 solar companies.

- The job market for PV installers is expected to grow 48 percent between 2023 and 2033. Experts believe more than 4,000 jobs will open each year.

A BRIGHT FUTURE IN CLEAN ENERGY

Jared Burns is a solar photovoltaic (PV) installer. *Solar* means something that comes from the sun. *Photovoltaic* refers to changing sunlight into electricity. A PV installer puts in PV systems. These systems create power from sunlight. They power homes and businesses.

Burns works for a solar company. His company designs and installs PV systems. It also checks on and repairs existing

Tape measures are useful tools for PV installers. Accurate measurements help make sure a solar panel fits correctly.

PV systems. Burns goes to homes and businesses. He works with a crew to put in PV systems. First, they mount solar panels on rooftops. Then they install other parts of the system. They run electrical wires between these parts. Finally, they connect the PV system to an electrical board.

Electrical boards have many wires that manage the flow of electricity.

The board is like a command center. It directs power to specific parts of a building.

Safety is vital. Burns tests the systems that he installs. He checks to make sure they meet building codes. Building codes are laws to ensure structures are safe. They make sure buildings are built to withstand natural disasters. This includes fires or floods.

Burns learned how to do his job while working at a solar company. He says, “You can do on-the-job training and get very far in this career.”[1] Burns says it is helpful to have certain skills. Installers should be good with details. They should understand how electricity works.

The job is also physically demanding. PV installers climb ladders. They lift

PV installers work with roofers to install solar panels.

heavy equipment. The job can be hard on a person's body. But Burns enjoys what he does. He says, "You get to work your whole mind and body every day."[2] He likes being outdoors. Installers also get to travel to different places. Burns says that he makes a good living. Best of all, his work helps the Earth. This is because solar power is a **clean energy** source.

Blue solar panels are made from polycrystalline silicon. They draw less energy from the sun than black solar panels, which are made from monocrystalline silicon.

CHAPTER ONE

WHAT DOES A SOLAR PHOTOVOLTAIC INSTALLER DO?

There are many tasks for PV installers. They design and put in PV systems. PV installers also repair systems and perform maintenance. Installer Kevin King says, “There’s a lot that goes into doing solar. It’s kind of like carpentry, roofing, and electrical, all in one.”[3]

When starting a project, PV installers visit the job site. They meet with the customer. They learn about the customer’s needs.

Work gloves, safety helmets, and glasses are essential tools that protect PV installers.

PV installers use software programs to help design different PV systems.

Small homes need less energy than large businesses. The PV installers measure the area where the solar panels will go. They find a spot that gets plenty of sunlight. PV installers also look for problems. A roof may not support the weight of solar panels. Trees may block the sun for part of the day. Shade reduces the amount of solar energy received. The PV installers must consider these issues. Then they come up with solutions.

After the visit, PV installers design a PV system off site. They choose a system that is the right size for the job. They figure out how much the system will cost. Then they send this information to the customer.

SOLAR SYSTEM EQUIPMENT

PV systems have several parts. All systems have solar panels and an inverter. Inverters turn electricity into a form usable in homes and businesses. Other parts include controllers, batteries, and electrical boards. These parts work together to create solar energy.

Solar panels are the backbone of a PV system. They are what absorb the sun's rays of light. They must get as much sunlight as possible to produce solar energy. Panels can be placed on roofs. The number of panels will vary from job to job. A medium-sized business could need seventy solar panels. But a small house could need only ten. Companies are researching more **efficient** panels. More efficient panels will provide greater energy with even fewer panels.

Every PV system must have an inverter. Solar panels provide direct current (DC) electricity. This current flows in only one direction. But most homes and businesses need alternating current (AC) electricity. This current changes directions. Solar energy must be changed from DC to AC. This is the job of an inverter.

A controller limits the amount of power that can reach a PV system.

Many PV systems have controllers. But they are not required. A controller manages the flow of power from solar panels and batteries. Sometimes panels get too much power from the sun. This extra power could flood a PV system and damage it. Controllers help prevent this from occurring.

PV systems may be off-grid. This means they are the home or business's only source of power. They are not connected to a **utility company**. Off-grid systems

Overcast or partly cloudy skies can decrease the sunlight a solar panel receives.

require batteries. Batteries store power until it is needed. When the sun is shining, solar panels generate electricity. Any extra electricity is stored in batteries.

Solar panels cannot generate energy at night. They also do not work in bad weather conditions. This is where batteries come in. They provide energy when the sun is gone.

Some PV systems are grid-tied. This means the system is tied to another source of energy. This source could be a utility company. Grid-tied systems do not need batteries. The utility company powers the building when solar energy cannot be created. But customers still may have extra solar energy when the sun is shining. Customers can sell extra solar energy to the utility company to earn money.

OFF-GRID VERSUS GRID-TIED SOLAR SYSTEMS

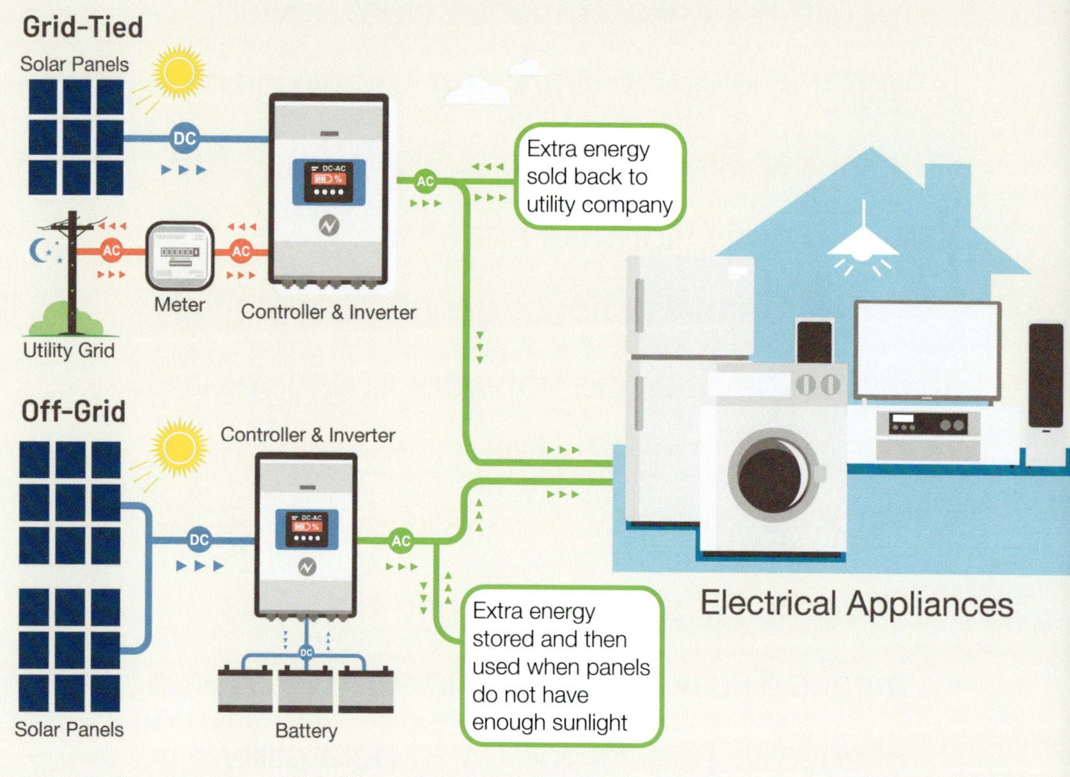

Solar panel systems store and use energy from the sun in different ways. This diagram shows the differences between off-grid and grid-tied solar systems.

ON THE JOB

Most PV installers work at homes or businesses. But some jobs are found at

Solar farms are put in open spaces.

solar farms. A solar farm is a giant PV system. It produces a lot of electricity using hundreds of solar panels. It can power many homes and businesses.

PV installers put in mounting systems at all job sites. These are also called racking systems. They are metal support structures for solar panels. PV installers may place these systems on roofs. They might also place them on the ground. PV installers mount solar panels to the racks. They make sure everything is firmly connected. This step is important because the panels are outside. It ensures the panels cannot blow away in the wind or wash away in a rainstorm.

Then PV installers put in the other parts of a PV system. They follow the design plan. They install the inverter. They may add a controller and batteries. Then they connect all the parts with electrical wires. These wires connect everything to an electrical board. The PV installers test the system to make sure it works. They do several rounds of safety checks.

Waterproofing is another important task. Water can get into solar equipment. It can

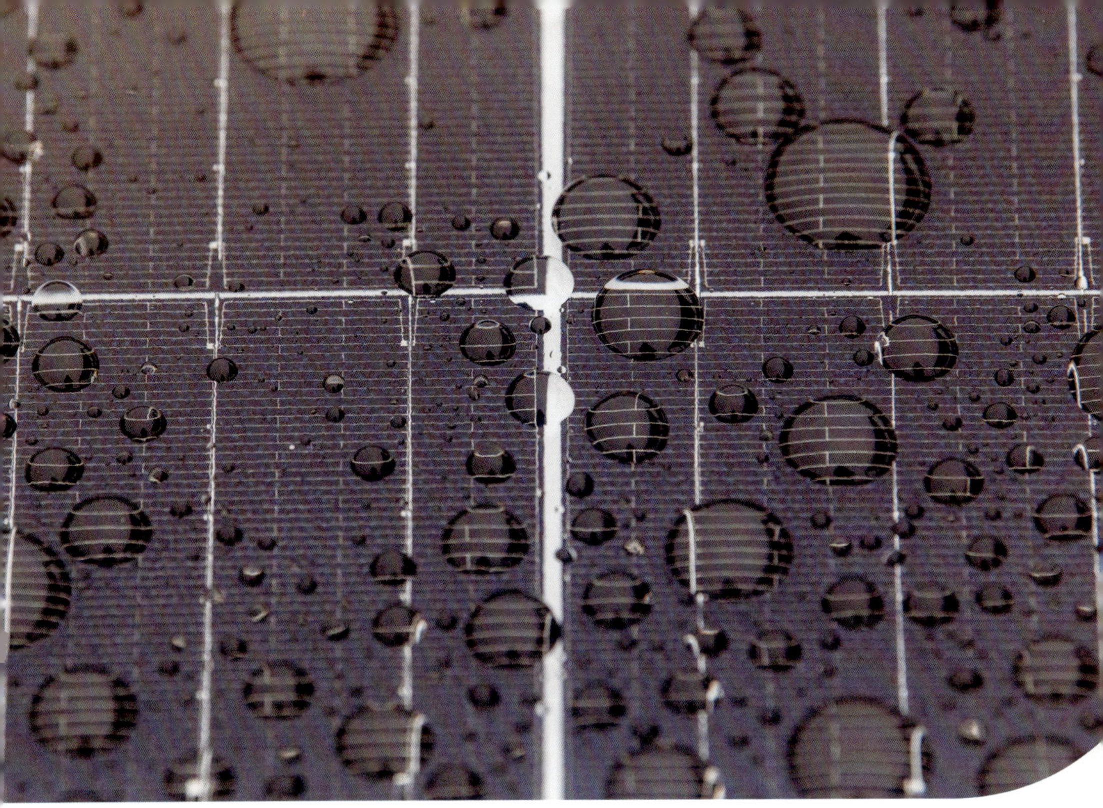

Rainwater can help wash dirt off solar panels.

damage buildings and PV systems. PV installers apply special materials to areas that might leak. These special materials are called **sealants**. They act like a raincoat to keep water out.

PV installers do check-ups. They inspect panels for cracks, breaks, or loose wires. They fix any problems that they find. PV installers also clean solar panels. A cleaning should be done every 6 months. Dirt blocks sunlight. It reduces the amount of power that a panel can make. Regular check-ups and cleanings can keep PV systems working well for many years.

BUILDING CODES

PV systems must meet building codes. Codes can vary by city, state, and country.

Using Drones

Sometimes PV installers need a clearer picture of a job site. PV installers often climb tall ladders to do their job. But this can be dangerous. A drone can do this risky work. A drone is a flying robot. It can fly high over a site. It often has cameras. It may have a special device that takes accurate measurements.

PV installers must research the right building codes for each job location. For example, building codes may say roofs must be very strong. They must be able to carry the weight of new solar panels. If the roof cannot hold solar panels, the roof may need to be repaired or replaced. There are other building codes, too. For example, PV systems cannot block firefighter entryways.

PV installers must ask for government permission to put in a new system. They must get a permit. This permit allows inspectors to visit a job site. Inspectors make sure new systems meet building codes.

CHAPTER TWO

BECOMING A SOLAR PHOTOVOLTAIC INSTALLER

There are several ways to become a PV installer. Some people take classes. Others learn on the job.

Some people enter the field with no experience. They find **entry-level** jobs as installers at a solar company. Then they train while they work. Others come to the career from similar fields, such as construction. Many useful skills transfer over. People learn other skills on the job.

Some PV installers may have started out working in the construction industry. They apply skills they have learned to become PV installers.

EDUCATION FOR PV INSTALLERS

PV installers do not need a college degree. But they should have a high school or General Educational Development (GED) diploma. Certain high school classes may be helpful for this work. These include science, math, and computer classes.

Students interested in solar energy may take classes about physics. Physics is the study of energy, matter, and motion.

Some schools offer classes on how to become PV installers. These include community colleges and trade schools. Clean energy groups also offer classes. These classes can be online, in person, or both. Most in-person classes have **hands-on** training.

Classes cover key information. Students learn about the parts of a PV system. They review how these parts work together. Students study off-grid and grid-tied setups. They learn about safety practices. Courses may also teach about the design of PV systems and ways to repair them.

TRAINING FOR PV INSTALLERS

The Solar Energy International (SEI) program offers in-person training. SEI students learn how to use power tools. They practice putting in racking systems. Students also install solar panels and other equipment. Then they test the systems to make sure they work. They also work with other students in the same program. They ask questions and take notes. They learn from teachers with experience in the field.

Some students who want to become PV installers have already gained basic skills at other jobs. They might be roofers, carpenters, or electricians. They know how to use power tools. They have helped build homes and businesses. Some have worked with electrical systems. Solar companies often hire people with these skills. The companies train them to become PV installers. But their training period

On-the-job training helps provide students with the experience needed to become PV installers.

is shorter. This is because they already have some of the needed experience.

There is a shortage of PV installers. More than half of solar companies say they cannot find experienced workers. Some solar companies hire people with little to no experience. These people have not taken classes on how to become PV installers.

PV installers must learn to effectively communicate. They work with many people in the field, including customers.

They have not worked in construction. These people are hired as entry-level installers. They learn and train as they work. Their training will take longer.

CERTIFICATION AND LICENSES

PV installers may get a solar certification. Certifications prove that a person can do a certain skill on a job. PV installers must first pass an exam to get certified. They must study a wide range of subjects. PV installers are tested on PV systems. They need to learn the right equipment to use and when. They should understand how to install PV systems, too. They must learn how to wire these systems. They should also know about safety practices and building codes.

Solar Ready Vets

Solar Ready Vets is a jobs training program for military veterans. It offers education and training to service members. It teaches them how to design, install, and repair PV systems. Then it helps these people find solar jobs when they leave the military. In 2022, the solar industry employed more than 20,000 veterans. This was 8 percent of all solar workers.

But the hard work often pays off. Certified PV installers may earn more money. The average salary increase is $11,000. Being certified can lead to other opportunities. Aaron Nichols got certified as a PV installer. Then he went into **marketing** for a solar company. He says, "The fact that I had the installer certification made clients in the solar industry especially excited to work with me on the marketing side."[4]

Several groups offer certifications. The North American Board of Certified Energy Practitioners (NABCEP) is one of them. This organization represents people who work in clean energy. It offers courses to help installers prepare for its exams. It also offers credentials for new installers. Credentials prove a person's qualifications

NABCEP certification exams consist of multiple-choice questions.

in a skill. A credential is easier to get than a certification. But it is still proof that a PV installer has learned basic job skills.

The Electronics Technicians Association (ETA) International is another clean energy group. It offers solar certifications. It also offers many courses for installers.

Electricians help manage and repair electrical systems. They often work with PV installers.

These courses help installers prepare for ETA's exams.

The makers of PV systems want installers to learn about their products. They offer free training. Companies teach installers how to use and repair their products. The companies give certifications.

Certifications are given by private groups. They are nice to have. But they are not required by law. Some states may want PV installers to have a license, too. A license is also proof that a worker can do a specific job. But a license comes from the government. It is required by law. PV installers should research whether they need a license in their state. Each state has different rules.

CHAPTER THREE

A DAY IN THE LIFE OF A SOLAR PHOTOVOLTAIC INSTALLER

There are many places that a PV installer can work. Sometimes they work with local customers. Other times they must travel. Their customers may be in cities or in the countryside. PV installers carry needed equipment for the job. This includes hand tools and power tools.

Most PV installers share similar duties. On a typical day, they analyze job sites. Then they help design and put in the

PV installers listen to customer needs. They build a good working relationship.

PV systems. They usually work on a small team.

ARRIVING TOGETHER

A PV installer's day begins early. The crew might meet at the warehouse. A team includes PV installers and construction workers. Everyone loads the PV system onto their vehicles. They make sure to bring the right tools. These may include drills, screwdrivers, and saws. Then the crew leaves for the job site.

One or more crew members speak to the customer at the job site. They go over what will happen that day. One PV installer says, "It's very important that [an installer] is going through the design with the customer . . .

[so] they know exactly what they are getting on their house."[5]

Safety always comes first. The PV installers make sure power to the home or business is turned off. They put on safety gear. Safety gear protects installers while

PV installers make sure to communicate tasks for the day with their team of workers.

they work, especially in high places such as on rooftops. PV installers set up ladders. They add ropes and **pulleys** to the roof for extra support. They make the work area as safe as possible. They may use yellow caution tape to mark the area. The crew must carry heavy equipment. They handle electrical wires. They must take care to keep each other and the public safe.

INSTALLING THE SYSTEM

The next step is to install the solar panels. PV installers measure the area where the panels will go. They make sure the panels will fit. They make any needed adjustments. Then they prepare the area with the needed equipment. They may add flashing to a roof. Flashing is a thin metal sheet. It helps keep

Solar panels are encased in a layer of tempered glass. This glass makes the panels durable.

water from leaking through the roof. Then they attach the racking system.

Next the solar panels are installed. The crew may need to use ropes and pulleys for high roofs. This is because solar panels are large and heavy. This equipment makes it safer to pull them up. Panels weigh between 40 and 50 pounds (18–22 kg). They are around 6 feet long and 3 feet wide

(1.8 m by 0.9 m). The crew mounts the panels on the racking system.

Then the crew adds other parts of the PV system. These include power wires that connect the system to the electrical board. A grid-tied system will be connected to a utility meter. An off-grid system will

PV installers double check to make sure all measurements are correct.

only be connected to batteries. Finally, PV installers test the new system. They check to see if it works. They make sure it meets building codes.

Once finished, the crew takes pictures of the finished job site. They write down a list of the system parts. This information will help if problems come up in the future. It can help with inspections. The crew leader talks to the customer. Then the crew cleans up. The job is done.

USEFUL SKILLS

People with certain skills are a good fit for the job. PV installers should like to work outdoors. PV installer Monique Flavell says, "Work environments can vary depending on weather conditions, so you are working in all different types of weather conditions."[6] Also, PV installers should not mind being high in the air. They spend a lot of time on rooftops. PV installers should be able to lift 50 pounds (22 kg) or more. They may have to carry solar panels and heavy equipment. They may need to go up and down ladders many times each day.

PV installers should like to work with people, too. They need to be able to

Working at Solar Farms

Most solar panels are placed on rooftops. But they stay on the ground at solar farms. PV installers help set them up alongside a crew of workers. PV installers help with maintenance repairs and cleaning, too.

When working on roofs, PV installers may use harnesses to make sure they are secure.

explain things to customers in a way that makes sense. They will also need to communicate directions to crew members. PV installers should have an eye for small details. They must be good at following instructions and making any needed adjustments.

THE OUTLOOK FOR SOLAR PHOTOVOLTAIC INSTALLERS

The solar job market is growing. PV installers will be needed to set up and repair solar panels. In 2024, the United States had more than 10,000 solar companies. More than 300,000 people worked for these companies. Half of them were PV installers.

The cost of solar panels has decreased over the years. More people may want to use solar power as an energy alternative.

PV installers clean the surfaces of solar panels with water, soft cloths, and brushes.

As solar technology changes, PV installers will also need to adapt and learn to apply new skills.

JOB GROWTH

Careers in energy and solar power have a bright future, especially for PV installers. The demand for solar workers will be high for the next decade. As installer Kevin King says, "So as long as the sun is there, we'll have jobs."[7] The job market for PV installers may grow 48 percent from 2023 to 2033. This means more than 4,000 new jobs could open for PV installers each year. The market for construction jobs is expected to grow only 6 percent during the same time. This means more solar jobs than construction jobs could open up. Many of

PV installers must stay up to date with solar technology and construction laws. By doing so, they help support the long-term use of solar energy.

these solar jobs are found in sunny states such as California, Texas, and Florida.

In 2023, PV installers made around $48,800 per year. A person's salary depends on where the job is located. It also depends on an installer's years of experience and skills. Experienced installers

Solar boats may help reduce water pollution.

made around $73,000. PV installers with less experience made around $38,000.

THE FUTURE OF SOLAR POWER

Vehicles have started to use solar power. Australia has a train that runs on solar energy. The train's cars have solar panels on their roofs. California is building its first high-speed trains. Officials hope to power the train engines with solar energy.

Some electric vehicles (EVs) have solar panels on their roofs. The panels help charge the cars' batteries. But the cars still need other sources of power. PV installers are putting in charging stations for EVs. Some charging stations are powered by solar panels on the roofs of homes or businesses.

Scientists are finding new ways to use solar energy. PV installers can work on

Solar Panels on Water

The number of solar farms is growing. But these farms take up a lot of land. Some companies are putting solar panels on water. Floating solar farms are efficient. This is because solar panels stay cooler and cleaner in water. They do not collect dirt. Putting solar farms on water frees up land for other things, too.

Scientists are working on developing cars powered by solar energy. These cars would not rely on fossil fuels.

Solar planes have large wings covered in solar panels to capture energy from the sun.

new products in the future as well. For example, some companies are working on solar windows. These windows have built-in solar panels. They take in energy from the sun when light passes through. Some companies think these windows will be popular. Many buildings do not have enough space on their roofs for solar panels. But they have lots of windows.

Some skyscrapers have hundreds of windows. Skyscrapers could become huge solar farms. PV installers will be needed to help make this happen.

Solar power provides people all over the world with clean energy.

Scientists have also invented solar roof tiles. Roofs would not need extra panels. The solar power would be built in. Scientists are also working on solar paint. This thin liquid would turn any surface into solar panels. It could be applied to the walls of a home.

Each new product may open new solar jobs and roles. This includes more PV installers. Solar marketer Aaron Nichols likes where the solar industry is going. "When I [see] the future of my solar career, it seems like the sky's the limit."[8]

GLOSSARY

clean energy

energy sources that produce little to no greenhouse gas emissions or pollutants

efficient

something done that does not take too much time or energy

entry-level

at the lowest level of a company or career

hands-on

having direct contact with something, or learning by being directly involved

marketing

promoting, advertising, and selling a product or service

pulleys

machines used for lifting heavy objects, made of wheels and ropes

sealants

materials that prevent liquids from getting through openings

utility company

an organization that provides the public with resources such as electricity, gas, or water

SOURCE NOTES

INTRODUCTION: A BRIGHT FUTURE IN CLEAN ENERGY

1. Jared Burns, "A Day in the Life of a Solar Power Technician," *YouTube,* uploaded by Indeed, February 6, 2024. www.youtube.com.

2. Burns, "A Day in the Life of a Solar Power Technician."

CHAPTER ONE: WHAT DOES A SOLAR PHOTOVOLTAIC INSTALLER DO?

3. Kevin King, "The Life of a Solar Panel Installer," *YouTube*, uploaded by Bloomberg News, September 16, 2021. www.youtube.com.

CHAPTER TWO: BECOMING A SOLAR PHOTOVOLTAIC INSTALLER

4. Quoted in Erin Greenawald, "Within a Year of Completing Solar-Installation Training, I Landed a Full-Time Job That Lets Me Live the Life I Want," *Business Insider,* July 1, 2024. www.businessinsider.com.

CHAPTER THREE: A DAY IN THE LIFE OF A SOLAR PHOTOVOLTAIC INSTALLER

5. "Typical Day of a Solar Installer," *YouTube,* uploaded by Mr. Jarrett, August 21, 2024. www.youtube.com.

6. Quoted in "Occupational Video - Solar Installer," *YouTube,* uploaded by alisWebsite, October 3, 2022. www.youtube.com.

CHAPTER FOUR: THE OUTLOOK FOR SOLAR PHOTOVOLTAIC INSTALLERS

7. King, "The Life of a Solar Panel Installer."

8. Quoted in Greenawald, "Within a Year of Completing Solar-Installation Training, I Landed a Full-Time Job That Lets Me Live the Life I Want."

FOR FURTHER RESEARCH

BOOKS

Emma Huddleston, *Become a Drone Pilot*. BrightPoint Press, 2021.

Laura Perdew, *Solar Power*. The Child's World, 2023.

Philip Wolny, *The Sun*. BrightPoint Press, 2023.

INTERNET SOURCES

"National Solar Licensing Database," *Interstate Renewable Energy Council*, n.d. https://irecusa.org.

"Solar Photovoltaic Installers," *US Bureau of Labor Statistics*, August 24, 2025. www.bls.gov.

"Solar State by State," *Solar Energy Industries Association*, n.d. https://seia.org.

WEBSITES

Interstate Renewable Energy Council (IREC)
https://irecusa.org

The IREC is a group that works with clean energy. Its website includes information about careers in solar energy. The organization connects job seekers and students with local training programs.

North American Board of Certified Energy Practitioners (NABCEP)
www.nabcep.org

The NABCEP is a clean energy group that offers certifications for solar workers. Its website offers programs that can help people get certifications.

Solar Energy International (SEI)
www.solarenergy.org

SEI is an organization that promotes solar energy. Its website offers classes with hands-on training. The website also offers courses that help installers earn NABCEP certifications. It offers classes for groups that are underrepresented in the solar industry as well.

INDEX

IMAGE CREDITS

Cover: © NF Stock/Shutterstock Images
5: © Aaaarianne/Shutterstock Images
7: © Anatoliy_Gleb/Shutterstock Images
8: © PV Productions/Shutterstock Images
10: © PeopleImages.com-Yuri A./Shutterstock Images
11: © nyker/Shutterstock Images
13: © Quality Stock Arts/Shutterstock Images
14: © DC Studio/Shutterstock Images
17: © Liudmyla Militsyna/Shutterstock Images
18: © Ahatmaker/Shutterstock Images
20 (grid-tied): © Allahfoto/Shutterstock Images
20 (off-grid): © Allahfoto/Shutterstock Images
21: © ultramansk/Shutterstock Images
23: © Sersoll/Shutterstock Images
27: © 1st footage/Shutterstock Images
28: © Monkey Business Images/Shutterstock Images
31: © goodluz/Shutterstock Images
32: © Sorapop Udomsri/Shutterstock Images
35: © EduLife Photos/Shutterstock Images
36: © Sirisak_Baokaew/Shutterstock Images
39: © Miriam Doerr Martin Frommherz/Shutterstock Images
41: © BigPixel Photo/Shutterstock Images
43: © kaninw/Shutterstock Images
44: © Rawpixels Stock/Shutterstock Images
47: © zstock/Shutterstock Images
49: © Somchai_Stock/Shutterstock Images
51: © Alpa Prod/Shutterstock Images
52: © MikeDotta/Shutterstock Images
54: © LouisLotterPhotography/Shutterstock Images
55: © Frederic Legrand-Comeo/Shutterstock Images
56: © Anatoliy_Gleb/Shutterstock Images

ABOUT THE AUTHOR

Miles Herman is a freelance writer living in upstate New York. In his spare time, he loves to research and write about trains and railroading.